This journal belongs to

Meghan Yuen

Introduction

Through my years in the fields of intuitive healing and human evolution, I have found colour to be the true expression of the human soul. Whenever I tune into people, the first thing I encounter is the various colours seeping through their aura and particular chakras. These shades of colour help me understand what's happening in the inner life of the person. I have always said the body doesn't lie.

Actually, the colours cascading from your soul are the most honest expression of how you are feeling, what you are thinking, how you are communicating to others and, of course, the state of your health.

We don't just see in colour; we feel in colour. Each colour emits a particular vibration that potentially enhances our inner life or drains it.

For instance, we know that green is healing, and whenever we may not feel well, we are drawn into nature. Somehow, we intuitively know that surrounded by the greenery of trees we are going to experience a sense of calm, regeneration and re-enlivening of our life force.

We also know that red can bring more aliveness, attention and circulation into our body. However, if we are feeling overwhelmed, angry or have a headache, then red could potentially intensify those sensations.

It can be fun to play with colour and see how it affects our energy, sleep and relationships. When it comes to healing, we need to become more conscious of when and how each colour can be most helpful. This journal offers you a space to explore and experiment so you can discover and refine your own colour recipes.

It is easy to work with colour everyday. Ask yourself how you are feeling and which colour will enhance your wellbeing. As you prepare for your day, consider which colour you can wear to bring more vibrancy to your life. What colour can you work with to enhance communication and connection with others? What colour can you use for pain relief or to help heal a part of your body? What colour can uplift your emotional state?

I've heard many incredible stories from people using a variety of wellness techniques and combining them with colours to help treat everything from back pain, carpel tunnel syndrome, sinus, throat and respiratory ailments, migraines, depression, reproductive issues and digestive difficulties to eyesight problems, sleep conditions and so many other diseases.

Taking responsibility for our own wellness is empowering. No one can guarantee physical healing, but when we take the time to tune in, understand what's going on and add colour to our healing regime, so much can open up.

Colour is all around us – every day, we choose what we put on and into our bodies. A green shirt and a pair of pants can make us feel entirely different than a red skirt and a yellow top. The clothes we put on, how we colour our hair, the jewellery we wear and even our makeup create a particular state of being.

The more in tune we are with our feelings, and the more we understand the healing qualities each colour possesses, the more sensitive and artistic we become in how we express ourselves. We then start to bring plants and paintings, furniture and decorations into our home to create a wonderfully supportive environment for our growth.

There are many ways to work with colour, from sitting in nature, to visualisation techniques, to energetic practices, to technologies that emit colour, to consuming a variety of foods, to working with crystals, painting, and doing movement practices such as eurythmy.

This journal will encourage you to bring more colour into your life and offer you various inspirations and ideas about how to become a more colourful, expressive person.

When I tune into someone and see bright, vivid colours in their body and soul, I know they are healthy and full of possibilities. Dark, gloomy, muddy colours indicate a lack of vitality and a tendency to sabotage one's growth.

When you start visualising colours, choose one and work with it for at least a few days to get to know it. Begin with very light, transparent hues and then slowly intensify the brightness. For more in-depth information on the benefits of each colour, explore *The Secret Language of Your Body* book or *The Secret Language of Colour Cards*. There is also a brief description of some colours in this journal.

May you discover all the beautiful shades within your soul.

Love,

Inna

Understanding More About Colour

Working with colour is not so much about visualising as perceiving a feeling the colour can offer you. Colour has the potential to awaken vitality or to lead you toward more pain and discomfort. The outcome can depend on your state of being before you start your colour work. Colour work can be like homeopathy, where less is more. For example ...

If you are feeling a bit low on energy, visualising, feeling, wearing or eating **red** may offer you a boost. Many people who become depressed are missing red from their aura, so adding it may bring some relief. However, you might want to avoid red if you are dealing with high blood pressure, headaches, anger or anxiety.

Use **green** to revitalise the nervous system. It helps lower blood pressure, calm the body and release frustration and anger. Green is also a comfort for heartbreak or hurt. When you don't know which colour best suits your need, use green as it supports whole-body healing. Too much green can over-energise the nervous system and encourage you to take steps you are not ready for.

Work with **blue** for throat and communication problems. It can aid in the decrease of fevers, reduce bleeding and soothe burns. Blue can help relieve headaches, release nervous tension and clear skin conditions. But, limit the use of blue for anyone with depression or circulatory problems.

Purple bolsters eye-sight, hearing and the sense of smell. It's a fantastic colour to use when working on inflammatory conditions such as arthritis. Limit the use of purple if you are feeling ungrounded and unbalanced.

Violet can aid in the treatment of insomnia, mental disorders, epilepsy and injuries that affect the brain. It also helps with diseases and injuries to the eyes. Violet can inspire the release of old patterns. However, too much violet may encourage erratic, unreliable behaviour.

Use **orange** for digestive ailments as well as chest and kidney disorders. It can support the treatment of asthma or other respiratory conditions. Orange improves immunity and vitality and awakens sexual and creative energy. However, orange can add to anxiety and intensify worry.

Pink is the energy of unconditional love. Use it to open and calm heart conditions. It promotes the gentle release of emotional challenges that relate to intimacy and restores tranquillity. Too much pink can be overemotional and controlling.

Yellow intensifies mental clarity and assists with cleansing toxicity from your intestines and bowels. It can complement the treatment of diabetes, arthritis and skin problems. However, use it sparingly as some find too much yellow overstimulates the system and fuels depression and exhaustion.

Use **white** for clarity and understanding. It is associated with purification and can help clear toxicity and feelings of shame, guilt or uncleanliness. Working with white may also improve skin conditions. Use white in combination with other colours, such as red or gold, to boost its effect. Too much white may lead to feeling depleted and washed out.

Gold can deepen your connection with divine wisdom and your soul. Use it to expand the nervous system. It is a strong colour for healing but must be used in small amounts as it is potent and can lead to overwhelm.

Silver is reassuring, calm and serene and thus supports the healing process. It can expand your awareness and deepen your insight into yourself and others. It can help flush toxins from the blood and tissues, and thus, boost kidney function. However, overexposure to silver may be linked to being emotionally unavailable.

Brown is grounding and can help you create healthy boundaries and think more realistically and practically. Use brown cautiously, as it can also drain energy and sap vitality.

Black can help you to dissolve and release the old so you can welcome the new. It's a gateway to new experiences and tests strength and resolve. Wearing black can improve confidence, but it is best in small doses. Too much black can drain you of energy and reinforce gloom and pessimism.

Various Ways to Work with Colour

Ask a question and allow a colour to come into your mind. Meditate on this colour. Focus on the sensations and the feelings it evokes. Does it make you feel cold, hot, lukewarm, more excited or calmer?

Ask which part of your body would like to experience this colour. Imagine a dropper that contains this colour in a very light form. Visualise squeezing out one drop and letting it move into that part of your body. Feel this drop penetrating as deep as your inner being can allow and creating a new environment inside you. The more sensitive you become, the more you will feel the subtle changes and the more options you will have to consciously create the type of inner atmosphere you would like to experience.

For instance, you may have felt hurt by someone you care about. By tuning in, you become aware that your heart has become hardened. You imagine squeezing a warm yellow drop of sunlight into your heart to dissolve the hardness.

You might read about yellow and what it helps with and choose to wear a yellow top. You might go to a park and find some yellow flowers to look at and smell as you allow their healing powers to work on you.

You may feel like you want to express this yellow light through artwork or movement. You might connect yellow to a song and put the song on and move around the room, exploring the warmth of that colour.

You can also take colour in through food and drink. For instance, if you need more energy, eat some strawberries. As you chew them, focus on the goodness that the red contains. If you want to work on your lungs, eat green lettuce and imagine this green light cleansing your chest and revitalising your lungs.

Placing or wearing crystals, which contain the colour you are working with, can also support your healing journey. Be aware that crystals can only work when you actively participate in your inner transformation.

I recommend using this journal with *The Secret Language of Your Body* book and *The Secret Language of Colour Cards*.

Questions and Answers About Colour Healing

How do I develop an intuitive connection with the colour?

Connect to a part of your body that feels tense. Do this by placing your hands on that part of your body and breathing into it. Ask your body to show you what colour it is emitting. Often, it will have dark or brownish undertones. Ask what colour would most support the healing and relaxation of this tension. When you sense or see the colour, write it down.

Ask if there is a colour that can hasten the healing. If so, write down that colour. You can send some drops of colour to that part of the body as described previously, or work energetically, using the following process.

> Think of a colour. Then rub your hands together for at least forty seconds and place them slightly apart. Imagine you are holding a ball of the desired colour. Feel the vibration of that ball of energy and explore it for a few minutes. If you are aware of the healing qualities the colour possesses, contemplate those properties. Then slowly bring your hands toward a part of your body where you have pain or tension. Breathe in the colour. Imagine the colour is moving through your body, purifying and strengthening it.

What colours should I be wearing?

Sometimes people get so comfortable with certain colours that they miss out on other vibrations and influences that could help change their lives. I see many people wearing black, grey and brown, and although these colours have their strengths, they can also create stagnation and drain energy when worn all the time. Think of all the ways you can bring more brightness to your life. When you wake up, ask yourself which colour could enhance your day. If possible, wear it, drink it, eat foods of that colour and meditate on it. Allow the colour to offer you more guidance during the day. If you have *The Secret Language of Colour Cards*, pick a daily card and do an activity associated with it.

Why do I sometimes react negatively to a colour?

When someone has an aversion to a colour, it is usually related to past experience. The colour may have been seen during and connected to an unpleasant event. Where this occurs, read about that colour and become aware of its qualities that might be helpful to you.

If you are uncomfortable wearing or visualising a colour, get a pen, pencil or marker of that colour and write with it. Write down why you don't like the colour and how it makes you feel. Often, acknowledging a difficult emotion can help release it and bring more colour and healing into your life.

Can I work with my kids with colour?

Yes! A fun thing to do with your children—who respond amazingly to colour—is to start playfully asking how they feel in terms of colour. For example, you can say, "If you could tell me how you feel right now through a colour, what would it be?"

Instead of encouraging them to use adult words, such as fear and anxiety, allowing your child to imaginatively explain their feelings can help them express and transform their emotional state. You might even ask them to change their feelings to another colour and see if their state adjusts.

Colour can also help a child relax, fall asleep, soothe something painful and become more creative.

Colour and the State of your Aura

This section explores the role of colour in evolution and behaviour. I could see auras and chakras from a young age, but when I came upon spiritual science, I recognised I could shape my organs of perception so I could accurately depict—in minute detail—what was really happening.

Over years of training and developing my senses, I realised that much of the information I was exposed to in the spiritual world was confusing due to a lack of research and understanding. We live in a world that is so focused on faster, easier, even instant access to information that we often don't recognise this way of living literally degenerates our body, soul and spirit.

The information below came through the incredibly evolved human being, Rudolf Steiner. Steiner was a great initiate and a prominent scientist. Steiner tried to create a synthesis between science and spirituality.

His philosophy of spiritual science sought to reveal hidden secrets of spiritual phenomena and help people to understand everything from the evolution of humanity and the hierarchy of heavenly beings, to homoeopathy, medicine, schooling, biodynamic farming, eurythmy, speech and pretty much every aspect of our lives. He is regarded as a highly accurate and progressive clairvoyant. His work has deeply inspired me to search, explore and deepen my inner life.

By working with processes that come from spiritual science, I have gained a greater understanding of what it takes to evolve and awaken our spiritual perceptions. While I wasn't lazy before, I now realise I took my abilities for granted. Rather than finding processes to polish my astral body and awaken my true organs of perception, I used what was given to me. But eventually, that became unbearable as I began to feel anxious, uncomfortable in my own skin, emotionally unstable and stuck. This led to what felt like a devastating inner breakdown and a very humbling dark night of the soul. I have worked diligently to purify and rebuild my inner life so that I would earn higher insights from the spiritual worlds rather than forcing an old ability from other incarnations. If you would like to enter deeper into this teaching, I encourage you to start with Theosophy.

Through Rudolf Steiner's work, I discovered that our auras contain three rays of particular colours. The first is denser and mist-like. The second is full of light. The third radiates a brilliant, sparkling quality. The first two rays pervade the aura with shades that remain more static, while the third ray is lively and full of buoyancy.

These colours intermingle inside the aura and are only perceptible to clairvoyants who diligently refine their inner organs of perception. Each aspect of the aura demonstrates what is going on inside a human being's body, soul and spirit.

The first, densest facet of the aura represents how the inner state of the body impacts the soul. The second, light-filled aspect demonstrates the soul and its level of refinement. The third, more active facet reveals the spirit's level of command over the more superficial, materialistic attachments and its capacity to access higher wisdom.

A highly skilled intuitive will perceive gaudy or murky colours, ranging from brownish-reddish to bluish-reddish in the first aura of a person who is absorbed in the selfish pursuit of desires, money and sensuality. This first ray of the aura will also reflect an individual's inner state of wellbeing: Muddy red demonstrates sexual craving and the quest for pleasure of all kinds. Laziness and boredom can emerge as muddy green. Trying to obtain a goal without the interest or capacity to do the work required surfaces in brownish and yellowish-olive hues. A mother's love and sacrifice, on the other hand, will surface in the first aura as a variation of shades between rose and light scarlet.

A focus on vanity, pride, ambition, eroticism, victimhood and untruthfulness will appear as muddy yellow to brown and dull and weaken the aura to such an extent that the second layer will only barely show tinges of brownish-orange colours. The third aura in a self-absorbed person will be almost imperceptible. Through a practice of meditation, purification of harmful emotions, refinement of concentration and the cultivation of profound thinking in every aspect of life, the first layer will become softer and fainter, while the second will expand and become filled with radiant, vibrant hues. The more a person grows in their understanding and service to all that is eternal in the higher worlds, the more their higher, divine self starts to exude that which is infinitely good, beautiful, true and righteous.

As someone develops their inner life and becomes more selfless, loving, wise, teachable, diligent and discerning, the stronger, more vivacious and enlightening their aura becomes.

When someone demonstrates intelligence and clear thinking, the hues of their second layer become pale green, while interest and an understanding of life and what is occurring at our level of evolution in the world turn the second layer a richer green. When someone develops their memory, yellow appears amidst the green. Pink indicates loving wisdom, while spiritual or religious devotion surfaces as blue. Indigo transpires when one can see life from an uplifted, evolved perspective.

When one's thinking focuses on the detailed understanding of the evolution of humanity, as well as the roles that divine beings play, the third aspect of the aura displays its splendour with light yellow gleams. A love for all beings appears as green but turns into blue if there is a willingness to sacrifice for the good of all. If a person then acts on this impulse and starts to actively perform acts of service for all humanity, like Gandhi, then their aura turns light violet.

A highly skilled clairvoyant or a student of initiation can look at your aura and see every thought, feeling and experience stored there. You literally become naked in front of them. This can be very humbling and may motivate you to become more mindful of your thoughts, feelings and, of course, actions.

Moreover, the way an aura appears to a clairvoyant will depend on their personality and their level of spiritual development. A person who is too focused on materialism will have cloud-like forms moving through their aura. On the other hand, a person who lives according to higher principles will have rays of light extending out from within.

Enjoy!

i think the rainbow of my day today was dejinetly a customer that complimented my style today! it seriosly made my day because i've been really trying to match my aura to my presence. how you present yourself i feel is very important! i've been super happy recently and i think it's because of chris and i's energy! he's so kind to me and it's so different?! i'm loving surrounding myself with people and things that deserve and appreciate my energy. honestly life slowly but surely is becoming better and better! rainbows are so perject because they only show after the storm... which literally represents my life. i now understand why and the lessons i learned from fighting my way through the storms. honesty i didn't deserve to fight that harsh and many times but the lessons i gained out of my storms are un-forgettabl.

— ♡.

A rainbow is a bridge to a mystical realm.

what the fuck... he just said he's going to show up with flowers on a rainy day. i can't ever recover from this. i'm not going to be able to sleep. god. i'm just so surprised... not complaining at all... man intrigues me. i'm just have never recieved flowers from a guy... especially not a good guy. i'm just in awe. bro, seriously the most perfect moment. he was just talking and i was listening to taylor, reading my guul plays and he just is so cute and flowers and he's like sunflowers like what in the fairy tale is going on? i'm so confused. no but seriously if he plays me i'll kill him, i'm not fit to be destroyed again, my heart can only handle so much :/ i'm just documenting this because it seems important and memorable. and now he's saying they'll be hand delivered what in the fucking gilmore girls... i'm internally and literally screaming right now, like bro, i'm too goofy and silly and indecisive

i can't handle this situation
but have seriously been longing
for this for so damn long. so
  i'm happy but what the fuck.
okay marry me i guess? no, too
goofy. ahhhhhh
  my dumb ass just tried to press
a home button on my phone...
bitch i'm so caught up in my own
world. god life is too good to be
true. god is playing me i swear
but he's so cool, funny. and
sweet. what the actual fuck.

october 26th, 2022

hey journal,
so, today is/was a different day...
chris hasn't texted me tonight and i don't
know what to do? like do i text him first?
he gives me such butterflies and i kinda
am just confused, nervous and questioning
all that is happening... i have absolutely no
idea what to do. i also just miss Europe
so so sooo much but also we're going
to disneyland so i'm super excited! i'm
just so fucking in love with Europe i can't
wait to go back! i'm going to die tomorrow
because i have my blood test and a dentist
appointment all in the same day... i'm supposed
to be meeting chris on sunday and i'm
trying to pretend i'm cool, calm, and
collected so that i actually am when i see
him in person. i'm just so super wanting
to take life one step at a time but i've
also not been this happy and excited in
a long long time. on sunday i need to
buy a new colouring book asap
because i god damn coloured my
other one really quickly. hopes are
trying to be stabbled right now.

In colour lives the expression of the human soul.

october 26th 2022

I love my work; I feel it's truly and really have put a good outlook on my life... I'm just so in the present and love it.

I feel like my aura lately has been radiating yellow; that's totally fun; and love cool!!

Recently got told that i remind them of fall time and that's literally the best compliment ever.

I ♡ being independant ← and adulting right now♡.

now i feel

I feel like happiness is radiant in me right now and I just want to give it to others, something I've never had.

↳ I love pampering myself now; clothing; morning showers; tea's are my reasons to wake up.

Recent obsessions;
· orange (burned)
· fall leaves
· smiling / laughing
· cats
· lana del queen♡
· fit pictures.
· Yolo/ life is just shits & giggles.
· flowers.
· poetry
· Books

<u>October 27th, 2022</u>

Hey journal,
 So, i'm shaking... so sorry if my writing is shaky, even though i'm literally talking/writing to myself. So... heart = broken.

I'm really trying to not let this situation to effect me too much.

I want to go back to Europe, I was happy there. I just want to be happy again.

Chris aka the Greek nice, funny, cool, and <u>GREEK</u> guy was going to get me flower... <u>Sunflowers</u> on sunday and now he's not. I'm really glad I made everything clear but also super sad that he's not looking for a relationship. But... I have to understand. He just got out of a long relationship and maybe he thinks they'll get back together? I don't know. He said he's just of "friendly guy" but... no boy buys a girl flowers without any romantic intentions... I don't know... I'm just sad he doesn't see me the same way... now I have to go through my healing era again. I mean I don't have to but I deleted instagram

Spoke to duck, going to ghost everyone, work my ass off, workout again, and read; draw ... restart. I'm happy I wasn't too invested but it's still really disappointing. maybe we will be together soon? or in the near future? Because he is super cool and funny...

Anyways, i'm excited to go back to Disney land but, I'm also craving to go back to Europe. I miss it so fucking much... I felt so happy and free there. I was just so super free. Everything was better there. But, healing before jumping into anything is a must do and I can't just skip steps of the healing process. I do desire a partner though... I'm hoping for one... but it's not a thing I truly need right now... my bad bitch/healing era is coming through now. Anyways, that's the update. Maybe my future Greek child will be reading this in our home in Greece.

Focuses (positive) — Benson ♡ disneyland in less than 2 weeks, morning showers, getting my nails done, reading, gilmore girls, art, painting, chapters colouring books, great coworkers, workout routine (rebuilding). ability to detatch from my phone, skin care to glow, planning Europe, travel.

I'm going to grow, heal, and find a healthy, loving relationship. ↓

I'm going to attract all positive guides in my life. ↑

PROCESS OF MY HEALING↗ ↗ healing relationships, and all things good.

I attract

Healing = discomfort, acceptance, growth.

↓ It's okay to love being alone.
↓
Fall in love with healing yourself.
⤷ don't focus on the hurt, you'll continue to suffer. If you focus on the lesson, you'll continue to grow.

I attract and radiate good, yellow aura, growth, glow, healthy relationships, and all positive things & people into my life.

⤷ I'm going to make all happy memories.

⤷ I am travelling and pursueing my dream life!

Awaken joy and enthusiasm with scarlet rays.

<u>Right now</u>

- I am ready for change
- I am ready to heal
- I am ready to let go.
- I am ready to attract positivity
- I am ready to attract healthy relationships
- I am ready to be happy.
- I am ready to find happiness within myself.
- I am ready for travel
- I am ready to find my destiny.
- I am ready for comfort
- I am ready for adventure
- I am ready for improvement
- I am ready for growth
- I am ready for the best version of myself.
- I am ready for my dreams to come-true.
- I am ready for beauty.
- I am ready to only see pure & beauty.
- I am ready to evolve.
- I am ready for a positive mindset.
- I am ready for my reason.
- I am ready for my highest self.
- I am ready to attract goodness
- I am ready to be seen as someone's everything.
- I am ready for healthy relationship
- I am ready for a loving relationship
- I am ready for more.

October 29. 2022

Hey journal,
So, sorry I missed a day... today I felt so so so
numb & drained... I had to say I'm sick today
and I feel sooo terrible for missing work,
but, I just couldn't. It's also supposed to snow
next week which is fun but I'm not ready for
fall to be over. I feel so stuck and mentally
and physically drained... I haven't even workout
in a long long time and I just feel so fucking
stuck. I'm dizzy & numb all the fucking
time. I can't cry. I feel like all my emotions
have been put on hold. I feel like every
day is the same. I know I leave for disneyland
in 9 days but I'm so numb it doesn't feel
real and I'm just feeling like I have no
time to truly process anything that's
been happening. I don't even feel like
I've processed Europe yet... I just never
feel extremly happy... except when Chris
was talking to me... he still is but, I know
he's healing from his breakup and isn't
ready but... I was just so invested. I feel
like everyone hates me but I have to remember
confidence is key to everything and nobody
hates me... nobody is truly concerned with

with me... truly I just need to relax... I just
need to fucking relax. I'm probably needing
a massage... I'm just truly unrelaxed. once
I'm away I'll feel better but I want to find
ease at being at home. I just find it relaxing
to imagine myself living laughing and loving
being in Europe... specifically Greece / London♥
I just crave living, falling in love, and marrying
a man in Europe. I'm meant to be there, to
create a life there. I don't know if I truly need
or want kids but I definetly want to find
love and have a bunch of cats and dogs!♥
Hopefully I find my soulmate that is cool
with that... I may even foster? I don't know...
I truly just don't want to live by the books...
I want adventure, I crave adventure, and I
want / crave change! I don't want to go to
school next year but... I need a stable
career... unless I marry rich?! High
possibility ☺ Halloween next year will
fucking rock though! This year is my
healing era ♥☺

Right now

- I have adventure
- I am confident
- I am exciting
- I am creating change
- I am travelling
- I am cool
- I am valued
- I am surrounded by only positive energy
- I have a healthy relationship
- I have positive, healthy friendships
- I am ready for comfort
- I am ready to find my destiny
- I am ready to heal
- I am ready to let go
- I am evolving
- I am smiling all the time
- I am happy
- I am my highest self.
- I am ready for a loving, healthy relationship
- I am ready for beauty
- I only see beauty in living
- I am ready to attract positivity
- I am ready for change.
- I am surrounded by kindness
- I am ready for compassion
- I am ready for more.

Watermelon is a colour of softness, gentleness and compassion
that encourages self-acceptance and kindness.

How I see colours

Red - fierce, firey, hot, confident, compassion, crisp, and softness.

orange - healthy, fresh, deep breaths, fun, jumping, fall time, pumpkins, feeling of calm, and adventure.

Yellow - radiant, bright, smily, air, laughing, positivity, adventure, crave, holding hands, independance, twinkle, eyes.

green - earth, nature, rain drops, fresh air, smiles, friendship, state of zen, adventure.

blue - ocean, water, sky, clouds, zen, yoga, genuine kindness, aloneness, good memories.

purple - softness, crave, romance, bubbly, mischief, crave for change, candles.

pink - light, fluffy, feathers, kindness, love, friendship, positivity.

white - empty, zen, calm, breath, open space.

Black - eary, forests, priority, loyalty, relationship, seriousness, fun.

October 30th 2022

Hey journal!
 So, today is the night before halloween!!! love love love! Ysabelle and I are going to dress up all euphoric and make spooky halloween charcuterie board and we're going to binge watch halloween spooky movies! super fun:) at least now my halloween will be all fun and spooky! we leave for disneyland sooo soon and I'm like not prepared, it feel so surreal. I can't wait for Ysabelle and I to get high, carve pumpkins, and take a ton of pictures! super exciting, I'm honestly not too excited for work tomorrow because I called in sick my last shift and Jen lowkey ghosted me, which is really unprofessional. It's giving me bowling alley flash backs. Anyways, let me just describe the spooky board because it may make me feel better... baked brie/w raspberry jam, chocolate covered almonds, cheese ; swiss crackers/fancy crackers, fruit; grapes; strawberries ! I'm super excited because I've been sorta deprived of social interactions... It's also supposed to snow next week... literally wtf. Chris; I agreed to build a snowman which is ultra epic yet, I think it'd be even cooler if we did it high ☺ Anyways, exciting stuff this coming week: disneyland ; house to myself ♡.

Right now

- I am ready for adventure
- I am ready for healthy relationships
- I am open to love
- I am ready for confidence
- I am ready for beauty
- I am ready to be valued.
- I am open to a loving relationship.
- I am open to positivity
- I attract positivity
- I am surrounded by kindness & love.
- I am ready for compassion
- I am valued
- I am creating change
- I am ready for change.
- I am ready for confidence.
- I have healthy & positive friendships
- I am ready for comfort
- I have achieved my dream body
- I am achieving all my goals
- I am only surrounded by positive energy.
- I have a radiant aura.
- I am healing
- I am evolving
- I am healthy & happy
- I am my highest self
- I am ready for more.

Hey journal,

So, I didn't write to you last night because it was halloween and I totally got fucked up with Ysabelle!! last night was so soso fun and it was so hilarious when we just started laughing out of nowhere?! Yesterday at work was actually fun with just Jen and we totally made the day go by really quickly! Dad bought an $8 scare crow which... he's so strange yet, silly. i'm so excited for Disney! 6 more days!! Also, fucking TayTay came out with her US tour dates but not her international... I don't know if I should buy my tickets for her vegas show or wait because... i may even be in Europe for when she's there! I would seriously fly anywhere to see the queen live ♡. saving all my money for her ♡. I need to start planning my Europe trip and book my ABBA tickets because your girl is not missing out on ABBA again! Europe is such beb and a safe place♡. okay, i kinda hate the ED clinic right now, I feel like they're pushing me out like tf? I thought they were supposed to help me... i mean I just feel like they're putting in less effort because they know i'll be out of the program. I don't know... I could be paranoid? I also haven't talked to Chris in 2 days and I kinda miss talking to him... Anyways, that's basically my life at the moment... Ellie is also taking me to Florence by Mills tomorrow and i'm so so excited ♡.

Right now

- I am ready for change
- I am open to adventure
- I am ready for confidence.
- I am open to positivity
- I am ready for love.
- I am open to love.
- I am valued.
- I am beautiful
- I am confident.
- I am ready for compassion.
- I am ready for a healthy relationship
- I am ready for healthy & positive friendships.
- I am achieving all my goals
- I am only surrounded by positive energy.
- I am radiating positive energy.
- I attract what I radiate.
- I radiate positive, warm & loving aura/energy.
- I am ready for comfort
- all my dreams are coming to reality
- I am healthy & happy.
- I am healing
- I am evolving
- I am my highest self
- I have a radiant aura
- I am ready for more.

November 3.2022

mission

Dear benson,
thank you for all. for being my light. You
can't read but it's the jus of it all.

Send pink into the hearts of all your loved ones.

Nov. 25. 2022

ok, so, let's pretend the last page wasn't me writing my suicide note - until I was inturupted. Anyways, I've been writing in my travel notebook because we just got back from Disneyland. so read that book for updates... I'm currently reading the book 'the subtle art of not giving a fuck.' It's so good and I'm not even on chapter 3. I've got now a lot of insight on how not to give a fuck, or more-so how to give a fuck in the correct way, about the correct things... It's a lot of "YOLO" philosophy. Honestly, I really needed to hear what the book had to say at this moment in my life (basically fait), because of how everything has been going lately. A lot happens in my head... A lot of thinking, sometimes a little too much. I'm currently giving my room a little spruce I've been putting off for so long and a lot has come to my attention. Like simply just moving my plants around, changing my books order/place, and rearranging my pin board - can do quite a bit for my outlook on my room....

I really am just stuck on school... like
I know I need it but a really big part of
me just wants to take another gap year,
travel a shit ton, stay at davidstea,
move into my own little apartement,
do what I love, yoga ; pilates every morning,
start kickboxing, paint ; draw, read
all the time, and then learn how to
open my own inn by taking a course
at the college in victoria... that's what
I really want to do... and the urge grows
more and more everyday. The only
thing is, is I don't know, and that's
kinda why im obsessed with the yolo
philosophy but, I'm just too scared ;
nervous to take that first step. which
literally defeats the entire purpose of
the yolo. I don't know, because going to
Thompson Rivers in the fall for psychology
and taking it from there doesn't sound
bad at all, because school is always
there. like it might be nice to test the
waters by taking a semester to see
if I not only like it there but also to see if
I'll enjoy that major. Plus, they have an
epic study abroad program.

kinda like the book said- we all give too many fucks- we all just need to start doing! And I want to just start doing! Not thinking too hard if it's rational or not. Like if I want to publish a book, then I'll do that, plus. if , and I mean going to school to test thing out doesn't sound terrible. It may even be good for distracting me from all the excitment I have about getting a breast reduction!!!, I'm sooooo excited♡. plus, if I fall in love with school and want to pursue art therapy, that's a good thing! and worst scenerio is that I don't like it, take time to travel, and learn how to open my own inn, or even find a new passion!? Either way I think I'll be happy with the outcome, we all die in the end anyways, so yolo♡

Magenta is the colour of deep inner knowing.

Hey journal,

So, i'm sitting here and watching my all-time favourite christmas show, dash & lily! I really would love to put a red notebook with the title "do you dare?" on a shelf in a random bookstore, awaiting for a teenage boy, that for some miracle actually reads and leave clues for him, if he'd dare he would try; solve the hints. I totally can but honestly I'm stuck on chris... for whatever reason he madly intrigues me. How can this boy not get bored of talking with me. I just don't know if this is strictly a friend thing or something else/more. I honestly can't read him... and I think that's what attracts me to him most.

If I were to start off with my #1 clue in the notebook — i would start off by asking/saying — if you're a teenage boy that has the urge to not be alone on christmas, you're welcome to take your chances and start by taking my clues... There are 3 books that represent me — these books will give you insight of who I really am... Solve these clues - #1)

I don't know - I feel like my book would go

EVERYTHING!

Something like that. Anyways, I go back to work tomorrow and I'm excited yet drained and dragging the feeling of starting life again. I feel the need to romanticise my life more, yet I don't know how. I need to ultimatly just continue to watch heart-wrenching shows and movies to romanticise my life, wishing I were in that land. Chris honestly reminds me a lot of dash... maybe just because I'm romanticizing everything, yet, he still continues to remind me of chris. I really hope to god that my feelings aren't onesided. I continue to be confused, rocky, and stuck with life. Anyways, I think that's all. Maybe I'm not the girl in his head, maybe he doesn't see me the way I see him, maybe he isn't good enough for me... I don't know?

Wear scarlet when you want to stand out and be noticed.

Visualise ruby to increase your stamina.

What m-

Still the 27th of
Nov. 2022.

I feel like I've got a ton of weight on my
shoulders and in my head... I feel like I need
to write all my emotions and every thought
in this notebook. I seriously need to get a
grip... I don't know. all I know is that I
am going to eat / or drink- I never know
what to say... Soup tonight. I for real need
to see some people ö I don't know?!
I want to go out and dance, party, spin
with ABBA blasting in the background...
and the only person I can truly imagine
doing it all with chris, I feel like we could
both teach each other how to have fun,
live life to the fullest, yolo at every chance
we could take? I don't know.

Here's to my unfinished thoughts....

Bring more sweetness into your life by indulging in some cherries.

Awaken your enthusiasm for life by concentrating on burgundy rays.

what Megran
needs

WHAT MEGHAN NEEDS.

money   5 greek men

A british greek man.

Brown is a colour of earthiness and a direct conduit to nature,
animal wisdom and universal wisdom.

December 9, 2022.

focus on the
now.

What i'm doing?

I don't know?

I need to regain focus.

focus on myself : work

you love
your job.

Contemplate life in a more realistic and practical manner with brown rays.

*Take your shoes off and stand on the ground, allowing yourself
to receive all the benefits of nature's healing.*

i have absolutely no idea what I'm doing...

is this what being in love feels like?
is this what I want to be doing?
Relationships are scary.
Growing up is really freaking scary.
Being an adult is really scary.
Being free is scary.
Decision making is scary.
Not being able to feel is scary.
Feeling too much is scary.
Not knowing the next move is scary.
Spending money is scary.
Focusing on 1 thing too much is scary.
Being loved is scary.
Having an addiction is scary.

EATING.

not eating is so powerful.
not eating makes me feel in-control.
being starved & sick to my stomach makes
me feel accomplished.
seeing my ribs & bones makes me -feel
productive.
rejecting food makes me feel in-power.
feeling dizzy, feels like I'm doing all right.
Restricting makes me feel like I'm doing
what I'm supposed to be doing.
Being worried about food, feels right.
Starving myself makes me feel at home.
Shrinking feels powerful.
feeling empty is powerful.
fading is powerful.
=

Being nourished is powerful.
eating is strong.
eating to be strong.
loving myself takes power & time.
allowing myself to eat is powerful.
Being stable is accomplishing
life is eating
food is life.
life is experiencing new foods.
allowing myself to fight the voices is power.

I want to be strong!

Working with blue creates healthy boundaries and balanced perspectives.

Indigo can complement the treatment of mental and emotional disorders,
such as ADD, anxiety and depression.

to be happy
a sugar daddy
talent
healing
1000 dogs aka
bees ♡
a life.
a new pen.
to be in Europe
a golf cart
a passion
a tan
✦ WHAT MEGHAN NEEDS ✦
to be skinny
to not be in depression
: money :
5 greek men
a husband
men to STFU
a british greek man
a new bed

Use bronze to break destructive emotional patterns, release irrational fears and anxieties and flush toxic thoughts and feelings out of your body.

Working with amber generates deeper bonds in relationships and allows you to express and receive affection.

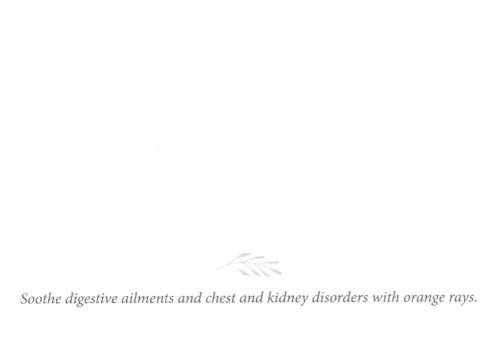

Soothe digestive ailments and chest and kidney disorders with orange rays.

Use orange rays to unveil your light and dark aspects.

Experiment with tangerine to awaken your creative juices.

*Imagine coral rays shining out of your heart, allowing more flow
and synchronicity in your life.*

Peach helps to soften any hard edges and imbue your etheric body with vital energy.

Apricot can lighten any heavy or burdensome energy you may be carrying.

Gold is a potent colour for healing. Use it wisely.

Ease arthritis, release toxicity and clear your skin with yellow.

Use yellow to step into the divine power of your higher self.

Warm your heart and soul with sunlit rays of golden light.

Use lemon when you are ready to think outside the box.

White represents purity, light, holiness, truth and surrender.

Pearl helps you develop clarity, integrity, truth and loyalty.

Black is a colour of protection, strength and retreat.

*Use black as a gateway to new experiences and when your strength
and resolve are tested.*

*Move through the black night of the soul. You will emerge wiser
and stronger on the other side.*

Use grey rays to identify blockages in your body or aura and receive insight
into your mental, emotional and physical states.

Use grey to give you an alternative point of view and provide you with strength when dealing with challenging situations that you feel are hopeless.

Emerald helps with overcoming fears, releasing frustration and creating calm.
Use emerald to transform conflict into compassion.

Emerald brings harmony to challenging situations.

Green revitalises your nervous system, heart, circulatory system and liver.

Surround anyone who is unwell with green.

Go out into nature and drink in the green lushness all around you,
awakening your connection to all living beings.

Jade creates balance, harmony and self-sufficiency.

Aqua creates a state of serenity, tranquillity and peace by soothing your mind and calming your nerves.

Aqua dissolves your fears to increase your confidence and self-belief.

Azure purifies your aura and strengthens your connection to the Divine.

Turquoise makes ancient wisdom accessible and provides a sense of connection to your inner mastery.

Build your confidence with the help of cyan.

Turquoise brings feelings into communication.

Blue activates your healing powers.

Use blue for headache relief.

Sapphire light can soothe your mind, calm your nerves and release emotional pain.

Purple helps with eyesight, hearing and bringing back a sense of smell.

Chocolate is a mixture of brown and black that links you to the earth,
provides grounding and encourages structure.

Use lavender to awaken your leadership qualities.

Plum is a colour of deep inner strength and faith.

Lilac is a soft, gentle colour that encourages you to expand your spiritual awareness and improve your connection to the Divine.

Use lilac to free yourself from old patterns and regain your inner power.

Mauve creates a sense of peace and tranquillity and awakens your inspiration.

Mauve improves your memory and ability to concentrate.

Lavender helps boost your immune system and assist with the healing process.

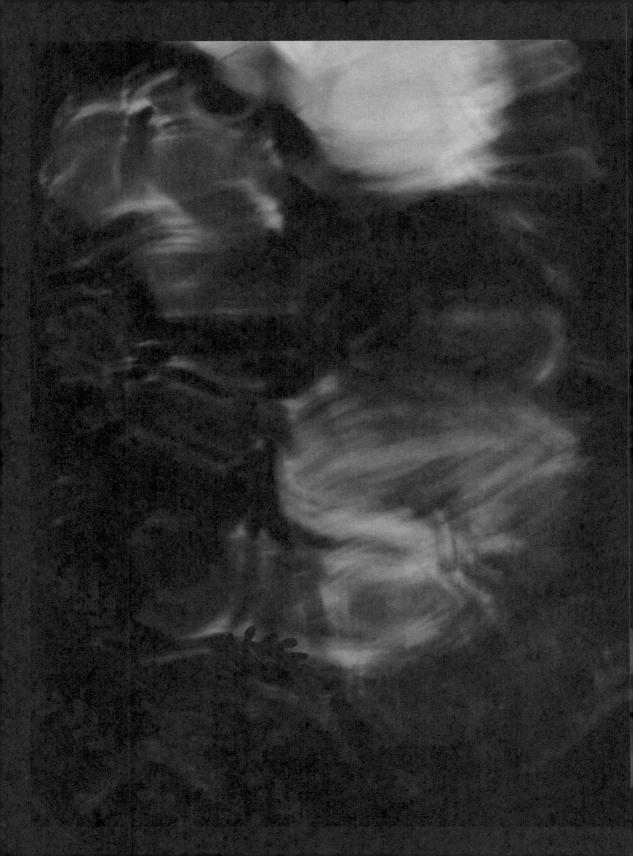

Plum can help you stay strong through hardships and difficult situations.

Release stale emotions with violet.

Work with violet to assist with any issues affecting the brain and the eyes.

Use violet before any prayer to enhance the experience.

Work with copper light to become more effective and efficient.

Use copper to help you lovingly express yourself in romantic situations.

At mealtimes, add a rainbow of colours to your plate.

Feel the healing vibration of each colour you work with.

Be conscious of how you think and feel, as this creates the colours of your aura.

*The more you work on evolving your intelligence, the more shimmering
shades of green appear in your aura.*

When you are practicing devotion, shades of blue emerge in your aura.

When you selflessly share higher wisdom, your aura lights up in
iridescent hues of red and blue.